I'll Forever Speak

ANNETTE ROBIN

WESTBOW
PRESS®
A DIVISION OF THOMAS NELSON
& ZONDERVAN

WestBow Press books may be ordered through booksellers or by contacting:

WestBow Press
A Division of Thomas Nelson & Zondervan
1663 Liberty Drive
Bloomington, IN 47403
www.westbowpress.com
844-714-3454

ISBN: 978-1-6642-4934-9 (sc)
ISBN: 978-1-6642-4935-6 (e)

Library of Congress Control Number: 2021922837

Print information available on the last page.

WestBow Press rev. date: 1/13/2022

Contents

Acknowledgments

I honor God and give him thanks for the opportunity and privilege in putting this book together. It would not be possible without him.

I thank my family for their love and support.

I wish to thank my son, Ramond Mangaroo, for his help with my book cover and photo display.

Thank you to my niece, Denise Hansen, and her husband, Chris Hansen, for making themselves available whenever needed.

Thanks to my church family of the First United Tabernacle International Ministry for their prayers and love.

Thanks to everyone on the publishing team of WestBow Press for your hard work and kind hospitality.

Thank you all. It is much appreciated. May God bless and keep you wrapped in his love.

Out of Sight

I dare to fly like a bird far away
From this place of misery.
Flapping my wings in saying goodbye,
I am hoping never to return.
Destined to find a relief mind,
Searching beyond the blue sky,
A place to call home
As I inhale the air with tranquility
And the thought of lifelong happiness.

Be Still

Broken and unspoken,
Isolated and infuriating,
Forsaken and forgotten.
Be still.

Weary and dreary,
Busted and disgusted,
Helpless and hopeless.
Be still.

Shattered and battered,
Despised and rejected,
Belittled and bewildered.
Be still.

Jesus is our Redeemer and Savior.
Bring it all to him and surrender.
He will fulfill our petition.
Just be still.

Bring down the Barriers

Tomorrow's youth hear my plea.
Let's unite and fight in making this a decree.
It's time to bring down the barriers.
We'll no longer sit and let the devil have us in bondage.
Let's bring down the barriers—
Barriers of addiction,
Barriers of depression,
Barriers of fear and insecurities.
Immobilizing our actions and stifling our true potential.
Let us rise with God's power and might.
Join forces, and get rid of the barriers.

Broken Bottles

Staggering and stuttering don't know my name.
Left alone, playing the same old game.
Broken bottles under my feet,
Up, down, and around the bend.
I need this charade to come to an end.
Broken bottles under my feet.
Taxi waiting, meter running in the heat.
They all gather, watching at me in the street,
Useless scumbag and pathetic,
Making a nuisance to society.
Broken bottles under my feet,
Stained with the odor of the intake of booze.
My life is unbalanced and incomplete.
Broken bottles under my feet.
Get me help, or it will be bittersweet.

Christmas

C—Is for Christ, conceived of a virgin woman.

H—Is for hallelujah; let the world sing and rejoice.

R—Is for righteous, which describes Christ's name and character.

I—Is for irresistible; no one can explain.

S—Is for stars that lead the wise men as they bear gifts from afar.

T—Is for the truth that announces his birth throughout the hills and valleys.

M—Is for the manger, where the babe was wrapped and laid to sleep.

A—Is for the angelic hosts who encamped as they kept watch over mother and child.

S—Is for the Savior who saves the whole world.

Hosanna and hail to the newborn King!

Come Alive, Zion

Arise, Zion.
Blow your trumpet, and make some noise.
It's time to come out of sleep,
No longer under the covers with your lights dimmed.
Arise, Zion.
Dressed in the right apparel,
Put on the helmet of knowledge for critical thinking.
Strap the sword of power around your waist to cut and clear every evil.
Anoint thy feet with oil to trample the enemy.
Ready, get set, and onward we march.

Arise, Zion.
Take everything by force and rejoice.
Light your lamps, we're no more in darkness.
Release the doors, open, and regain every lost soul.
We are ready to worship the King.
Long live Zion.

Day of Fast

Turn down the plates.
Disconnect the television.
Mute the phones.
Let's come with a focus in mind,
To be purged from the sins of this world.
Bow down and worship him.

Abstain from gossip.
Refrain from profanity.
Walk in purpose and with obedience.
Feast your eyes on the things above.
Give glory to his name.

Gather to feed the hungry.
Rescue the poor and needy.
Embrace our sisters and brothers.
Sing unto him with the voice of a psalm.
Let our praises heard on high.

It's the day of fast.
Let's study his Holy Word.
Pray without ceasing.
We have come to break every chain
To gain back that which was stolen,
To decree and declare our blessings from the Lord
For he is the king of kings.

Dismayed

Don't be dismayed
If there's never a song on your
Lips to sing.
Don't be dismayed
If life's journey seems to wear you out.
Don't be dismayed
If at times your mind is filled with doubts.
Don't be dismayed
If there's no money to put food on the table.
Don't be dismayed
If you're lonely and troubled.
Don't be dismayed
In all that you do, and no matter life's challenges.
Just remember: God will take care of you.

Hope

Hope is what keeps our minds at ease.
To hope in God brings you to a place of peace.
Hope turns worst into the best.
To hope in God will help you to conquer each test.
Hope teaches patience when your back is against
The wall.
To hope in God will keep you from Satan's falls.
Hope destroys the uncertainty of life.
To hope in God will release you from
Bitterness and strife.
Hope overcomes the puzzles and mysteries.
To hope in God guides you through life's struggles.
Hope encourages us on our never-ending journeys.
To hope in God we will have his truth and not a story.
Hope never fails when you are determined.
To hope in God gives you the confidence to trust
And to receive the richness of God's eternity.

Excuses

An excuse is a part of our everyday expression,
Constantly at the drop of a hat,
No matter how it is used or said.
Excuses at times can be unreasonable and inexcusable.
Don't assume you are not capable of handling any given task.
Life is a mystery and a journey we must all take without the excuses.
I have spoken, so now may I be excused?

Food for Thought

The spirit of God is righteousness,
Purity,
Patience,
Respect,
Trustworthiness,
Faithfulness,
Obedience,
Humbleness,
Self-control,
Kindness,
Loyalty,
Perseverance,
Unity,
And above all, he is love.

God Don't Like Ugly

Scheming and plotting,
Observing the righteous,
Heart consumed with hatred and jealousy,
Eating away like maggots.
Mind tormented; can't find relief.
Vicious, devious, and ruthless,
Like a lion waits to make his pounce.
Feeling empowered by your eager,
Hiding in the dark.
Wow, be unto you, old dragon.
Your days will come to an end.
The wrath of God will demolish you
For God don't like ugly.

His Decision

Often we search all over in finding answers for our questions.
But we know that doesn't always happen.
The truth of the fact is that Jesus knows it all.
What will you do when you pray to God about a situation,
And he says, "Wait"?
Will you have a tantrum and run to your room with doors shut?
What happens when God says, "Wait"?
Will you turn your back on him with a frown?
Frustration and confusion lie in your path,
And still he utters the word, "Wait!"
Will you give him a piece of your mind?

The days, weeks, and months have gone by, and in the midst
His reply to you is waiting!
Will you pack your bags to hit the road?
What happens when God says, "Wait"?
Will you stop your worship and praise?
No matter what we do or what we say,
God's timing will always matter.
If he is the one in charge and with a plan for our lives,
Then, therefore, we have to wait.

The Intimacy of the Heart

Prayers should be practice as an everyday lifestyle attitude.
Without it, we are lifeless.
Prayers are the most fundamental source to a lifeline connection
To the Holy Spirit.
In times of temptation, challenges, and tragic experiences,
It is a lifesaver.
Prayers must be in sincerity and of love, knowing
We have a lifelong friend whose name is Jesus.

Invasion

On a mission proclaiming God's truth,
Beaten, battered, and bruised,
They want me to quit.
But I refuse to submit.
Throw me in the dark and filthy pit,
I will not be afraid of their weapons
For in God I trust.
And in the stillness of the night,
I'll offer to him all my worship
As he watches from heavens above.
Sends forth his angels to rescue me,
No longer a captive but free.

Judge Not

You dare not look at me to judge,
Nor to speak negative things about me
For you know not who I am.
My clothes may not be of designer wear but the thrift shop.
Working endlessly, trying to survive, caring for my brothers and sisters.
Life for me was no easy streets, and I certainly never had the privilege
To dine at the finest of restaurants, eating filet mignons.

Some guys have all the luck, and some don't.
But no matter what life throws out,
You have to move on.
I don't drive around in a Cougar but use my blessed feet.
You cast your eyes and turn up your nose,
Scrutinizing and criticizing as if you are all that.
How dare you judge me?

Words are strong, and it's oftentimes said
It's not the cover of the book but the story.
So rude and no respect,
Slamming the door in my face,
Leaving me standing as if I am some kind of reject.
Laughing and talking with your friends about me.
So fortunate some of us were born with a gold spoon in our mouths.
Get over yourself.
We all are God's handiwork, and he loves us all.
Next time you decide to pass judgment,
Take time out to know who I am.
You may want to call me a friend.

Just a Prayer

Father, I come before you with my sins.
Please forgive me for all that I did wrong.
My life has spun out of control,
And at times, I can hardly find my way.
So hear my humble cry.
I am a burden without rest.
My eyes have swollen from my tears.
Look down and save me.
I am longing for my soul to be right.
Lead me to that glow of a light.
This my solemn prayer unto thee.
I am sincerely on bended knees.
In God I trust never to leave me alone.
Dearest Lord, don't hide your face from me.

Land of the Dead

Tucked in, eyes all tightly shut.
Doors locked, and no one will knock.
Neighbors around, don't speak, hear, nor see.
Beds layered and decked with flowers of all blooms.
Names in print with words of kindness too.
It's bedtime, and we are all asleep.
Silence lives around us from day to day.
We don't work, nor do we play.
Free from pain, sorrows, and life that comes with many challenges,
No longer deemed at making choices.
And now, if you would, excuse us please.
We are not open to suggestion but only
Remembrance.
Goodbye, farewell, and good night.

Lift Him Up

Let our praises to him be in abundance.
One that sends chills to his spine,
A bubble of joy to his heart,
And the satisfaction of great admiration.
Let his Shekinah glory
Fall from high,
Touching every man, woman, girl, and boy
For his name to be praise.
Let the seas and the flood resound
That shows thankfulness for his creation.
How great is the Lord of all.
He is worth being praised.

Mindset

A renewed mind speaks with authority.
A renewed mind walks in dominion.
A renewed mind abstains from evil.
A renewed mind lives in obedience.
A renewed mind stands for the truth.
A renewed mind is earnest in prayer.
A renewed mind is content.
A renewed mind is humility.
A renewed mind is of peace.
A renewed mind grows to maturity.
A renewed mind is forgiveness.
A renewed mind proclaims the name of Jesus.
A renewed mind is the opportunity in which all things
Are passed away, and all things have become anew.

One Touch

A woman of many years
Who had an infirmity
Traveled near and far with anxiety
In search of finding relief and a sense of peace.
But when she saw the Master of great wonders,
She pushed onward with exhaustion and a will of determination.
Paying no attention to anyone's words or actions,
Her frail hands outstretched and touched his garment.
Then suddenly, she was healed.
How good it felt to experience such a miracle, testimony, an authentic
story.

Pain

It slithers like a snake in the grass,
Moving throughout my extremities,
Striking without warning and thoughts of
How long it will last.
Tossing and turning and unable to escape the
Intensity and excruciating agony that it brings,
Preventing me from being still.
Powerless, speechless, and about to lose my mind,
The weakness of my body can no longer coincide.
Mercy is all I need to make it through.
"Take your flight, I now command you.
You have been working overtime.
I no longer accommodate you
Pain, pain go away.
The Spirit of the Lord rebukes you."

Questions

The whys become hows.
The yeses become nos.
The adventures become tragedy.
The love becomes hatred.
The dos become don'ts.
The haves becomes have-nots.
It's a world filled with questions
With no answers as to what should be.
Knowing that life is for living,
And death becomes silent without the questions.

Keeping It Real

Stand for who you are.
Don't fake it to make it.
Display the qualities you have.
Forget about every critic;
Don't try to please.
Embrace your true identity with ease.

Appreciate the things you can accomplish.
Waste no time on what you can't fix.
Be happy, and live each day anew.
Focus on where God wants you to be
As tomorrow is guaranteed only to a few.

Grab hold of self-confidence.
Ignore the haters and accusers.
And in whatever you do,
Remember: no one is more important
Than you.

She-Devil

She saintly walks along her path,
Feasting her eyes on who she may devour.
Wearing clothes of crimson shade,
Is veiled as to hide her identity.
She takes her seat in the darkest corner of the room,
Licking at her lips with an appetite large.
Anxiously waits to spew the venom of seduction
While she lures her victim away unnoticed.
A mind filled with evil plans,
She will stop at nothing to have her way—
No matter the cost.
Aiming to destroy the innocent
Who has done her no harm.
One by one she accomplishes her task,
Feeling mighty and in control.
She leaves no trail as she takes her flight.
Nobody sees where she goes,
But someday she'll be defeated.

Sorry

Stubborn and selfish,
Wrestling with the thought of deleting it from the mind.
It has to be heard and not said;
A simple apology makes a difference.
Being responsible and owning up to your action
Alleviate selfishness and pride.
Unburdening the load of guilt,
Leaving all conscience-free and clear.
So the next time you do something unacceptable,
Don't stutter; be bold to say out loud,
"Sorry!"

Sunny Day

Peeping through the clouds from above,
Descending with gleam,
Bursting heat spreads over the fields of green.
Butterflies flutter with their beautiful colors.
Birds are chirping around in such splendor.
Children at play with the joy of delight
As the sun shone, making the day so bright.
Lilies and daffodils are in bloom.
Rivers overflow, casting their shadows over the hills and
Mountains.
It pierces through the stained-glass windows with
Reflection of rainbows,
This spherical shape from heavens creation

The Cross

How can I forget the blood-stained cross?
On it, he died to pardon me
From a life of sin and shame.
Took away his dignity,
Smeared his character.
What indigenous plight in our sight.
But in my heart I know he'll forever reign.
I'll remember the cross of Calvary.

The Eyes

They follow your every move.
Watching keenly everything you do
From dawn till dusk,
Seeing the good and bad.
Eyes of seduction and lust,
Looking at the things of the world.
Eyes in comprehensive gaze, filled with curiosity.

Sad eyes and unseeing eyes,
Penetrating, intensifying, making you uneasy.
They come in pairs and, at times, fours.
Sights, all around.
What they see nobody knows.
Hidden and at watch,
Peeping through to get a glimpse.
Stopping at nothing to be enthused.
Eyes of colors at a distance
Soon get tired and shut.

The Glory

The physical minds of humans cannot grasp the understanding of the existence of God's glory.

The awesomeness and wonders marvel them.

God's omnipotence moves upon and over the circumference of the earth,

Changing the imperfect to perfection.

This infinite God, who created all beings,

Orchestrates the nonvisible to visible.

It's distinct.

It's divine.

It's honorable.

That's the glory of God.

God's Helper

God's helper
Must have a mind to serve.
Faithful and committed,
Binding the threats of the enemy.

God's helper
Must walk in a humble way,
Demonstrating righteousness,
Not compromising the truth about the doctrine.

God's helper
Must have an ear to hear
Preaching the Word in and out of season,
With the ability to receive and declare that of the Lord.

God's helper
Must seek out the lost,
Aiding the poor and needy.
Laying of hands in healing the sick.

God's helper
Must possess clean hands
And a pure heart.
Stay bounding in the Word of the Lord.
God's helper
Must be prayerful,
Winning souls for God's kingdom
No matter the cost.

God's helper
Must respond to the call to go far and beyond,
Not with fear and trembling,
But with boldness and power,
Keeping the fire of the Spirit burning.

The Promise Keeper

Trials and struggles come your way.
And it seems as if you are heading for a downfall.
Remember: I am your strength.

When the doctor's report seems unfavorable,
And there is nothing else to do,
Remember: I am the way maker.

If rejected and feeling alone
And no one to call a friend,
Remember: I will never leave you nor forsake you.
Hungry and homeless,
Clothes in rags,
Remember: I'll supply your needs.

When your enemies rise against you
And want you out cold,
Remember: the battle is not yours,
It's mine, the Lord's.
And if there's ever a time
You can't find words to say,
Remember how I taught you to pray,
"Our Father who art in heaven,
Hallowed be thy name,
Thy kingdom come,
Thy will be done,
On earth has it is in heaven.
Give us this day our daily bread,
And forgive us of our trespasses
As we forgive those who trespass against us.

And deliver us from all evil
For thy is the kingdom
The power and the glory
Forever and ever—Amen." (Matthew 6:9–13)

The World

Chaos, disruption, tumult, danger, commotion,
Storms, earthquakes, tornadoes, and eruptions.
Earth's natural disasters, all works of fate.
Man aided with a quest to dominate,
Never counting species that we eliminate.

Wars, sickness, and great pandemics,
Shootings, stabbings, buildings going up in smoke
Causing catastrophes and human losses,
Living in fear and running scared.
Trust, confidence, and brotherhood no longer exist.

Compassion is lacking, and empathy's gone.
No one cares if you live or die anymore.
We're all in a rat race, against all odds,
Thinking and believing that we're little gods.
It's about me, me, and me.
Sparing not a moment to worry for the other guy.
What's wrong with the world?

Who Is God to Us?

Who is God to us?
Is he a figment of our imaginations?
A character we read about in a storybook
When we were children?

Who is God to us?
A longtime friend we accidentally bumped
Into to have a quick chat,
Exchange numbers, and waved goodbye.

Who is God to us?
A chore on our list of things to do
With the assumption that one day
It will get done.

Who is God to us?
Is he a math theory we can't solve,
Frustrated and tired,
Call it quits, and ready to move on?

Who is God to us?
Isn't he the Creator of the universe?
Shanika glory,
Sovereign
Savior, Lord, and King.
That's who he is.

Food For Thought -2

Be polite to those you meet
Be respectful to those you serve
Be patient in wanting and waiting
Be positive in the things you do
Be true to one-self
Be appreciative of life
In all you do, avoid all murmurs and complaints.

Untitled

The Word of God is our daily bread
That does not require buttering.
In reading, leaves you touched, moved, and inspired.
This book is no ordinary book;
It will lead us to all truth.
Living committed in total submission,
Walking in God's divine path,
Allowing the world to see
The reflection of God's light in you.

You Deserve It- (That Love)

There are things in life you want for yourself.

But, there are also things in life you dream about for someone else

When I wish and wonder, amazingly, I look no further as to ponder

I found out that person to be you

Even though I might not know everything about you that I need to know, but more importantly, I found out who you are.

God design you to be remarkable, articulate, assertive, nurturing, bold, and one that is appreciated by many.

And above that, he has given you a love that will fill your heart with joy and happiness.

He has created a life of prosperity that you will triumph in every sense of the way

Life of an opportunity that you will take without fear

Life of duties for you to perform till the end

Life of beauty that reflects who he is

And if there is anything else,

I genuinely have left, that I must say,

It all sums up to you deserve it.

Prayer of Thanks

Father above, we thank you for your breath
Bless and take care of all those in need
Give them strength from day today
Be their compass and guide them every step of the way.
Don't let them lose hope or be afraid.

Father above, we thank you for the many provision
Never less our many dissatisfactions
Teach us to humbly and move on
For you have been a loving Savior and
good friend

And as we continue to walk this path of life
Keep our minds that we will last
Let us know right from wrong
Thank you, God, for everything.

Printed in the United States
by Baker & Taylor Publisher Services